Back to Basics

MATHS

for 5-6 year olds

BOOK ONE

George Rodda

1 one   2 two

1 | | | | | 2 2 2 2 2

Draw round

1 dog

2 cats

1 mouse

2 birds

1
one   one   one   one

2
two   two   two   two

Count how many

- [2] eggs
- [ ] knives
- [ ] spoon
- [ ] mug
- [ ] egg cups
- [ ] buns

Draw and colour

2 spoons

2 mugs   1 bun

Draw round

3 ducks    3 trees

   3 rabbits

   3 flowers

Count how many

3 balls
☐ books
☐ dolls
☐ kites

Draw 3 balls

Draw 3 kites

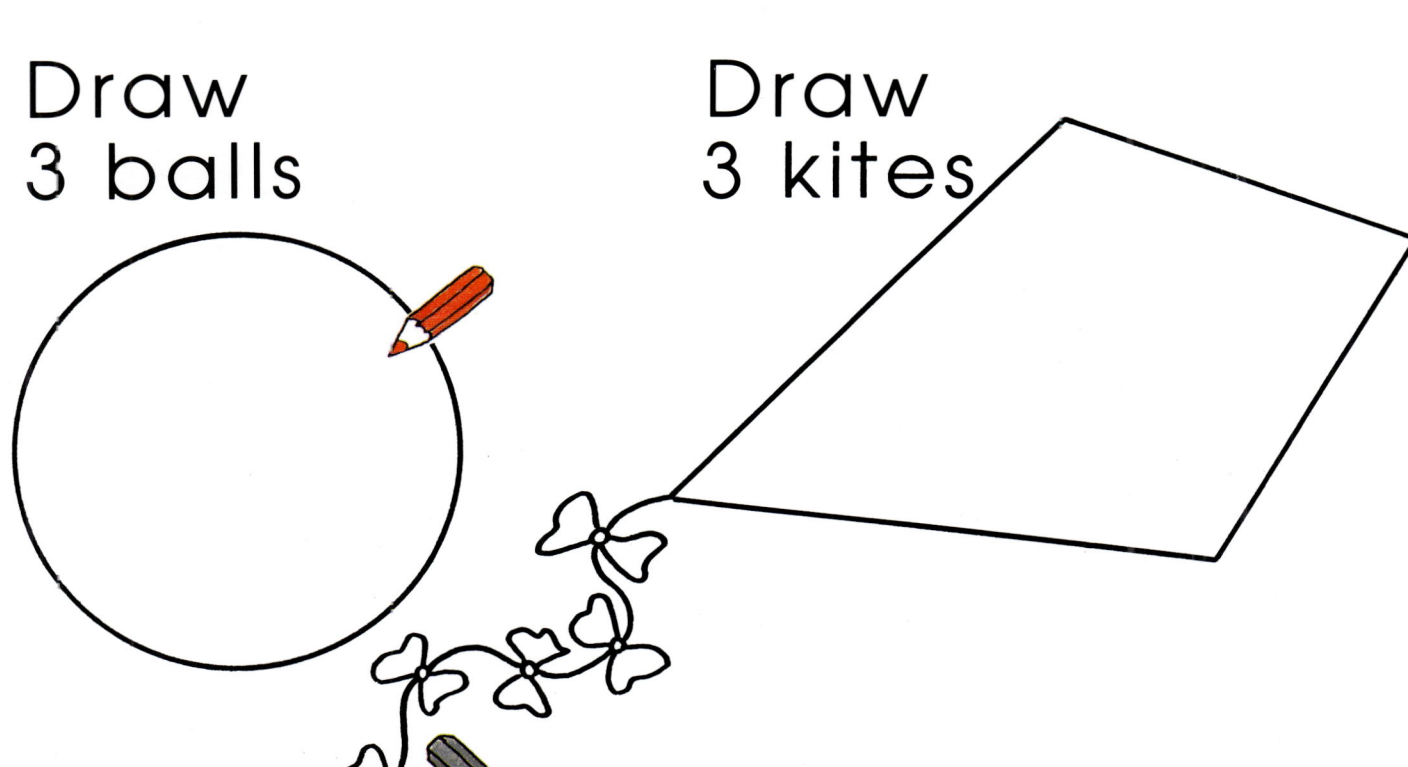

three three three

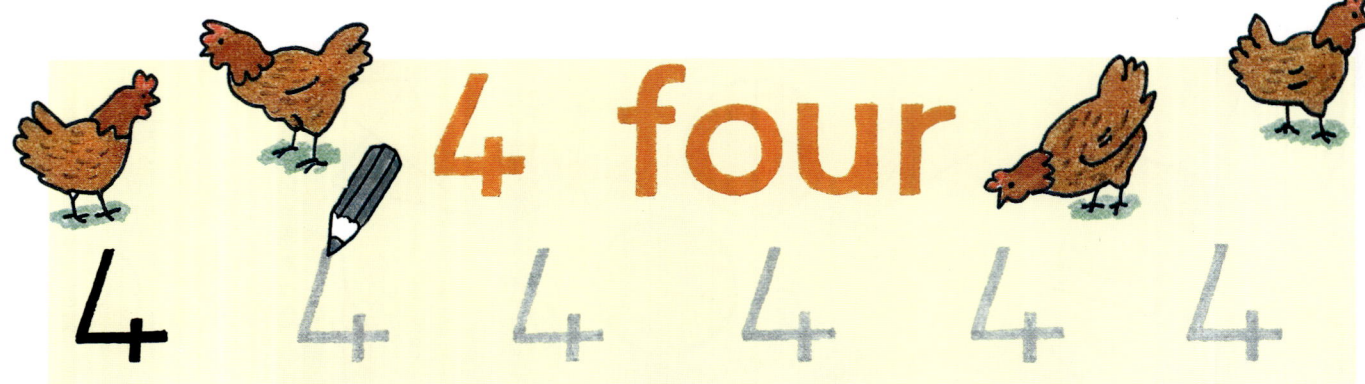

4 four

Count how many

☐ horses ☐ cows

☐ sheep ☐ hens

four   four   four

four   four   four

Draw

4 red apples

4 trees

4 houses

one 1 2 3 4

two

three

1 2 3 4 four

Count how many

1

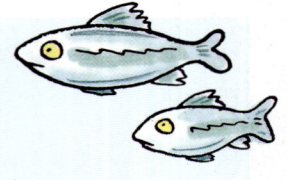

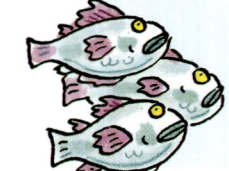

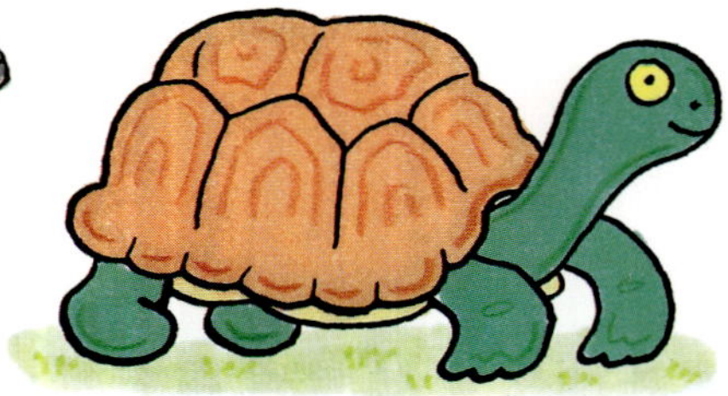

one

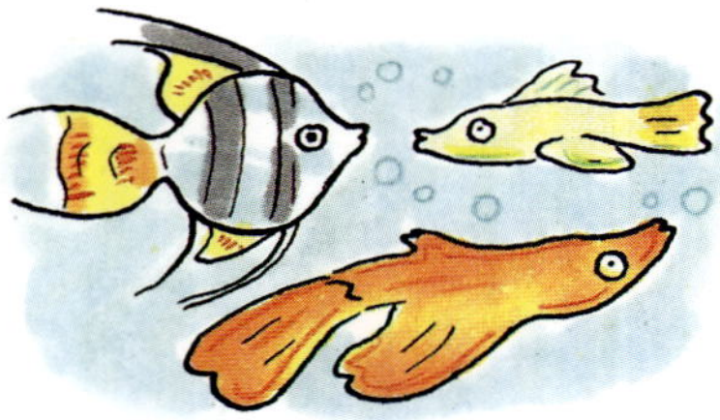

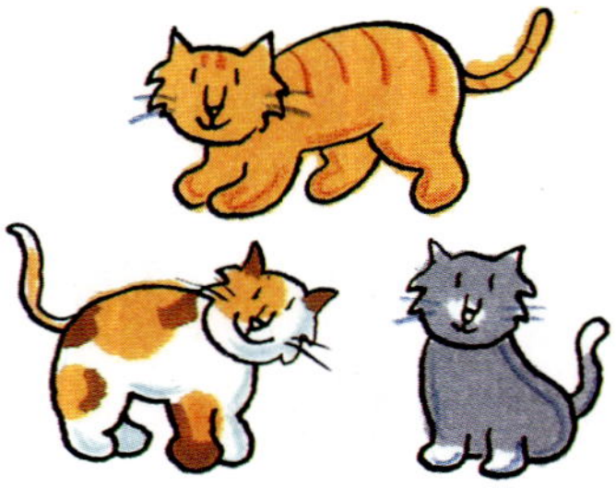

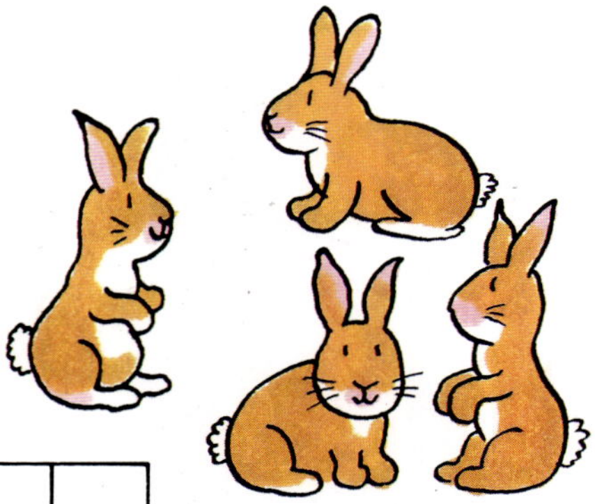

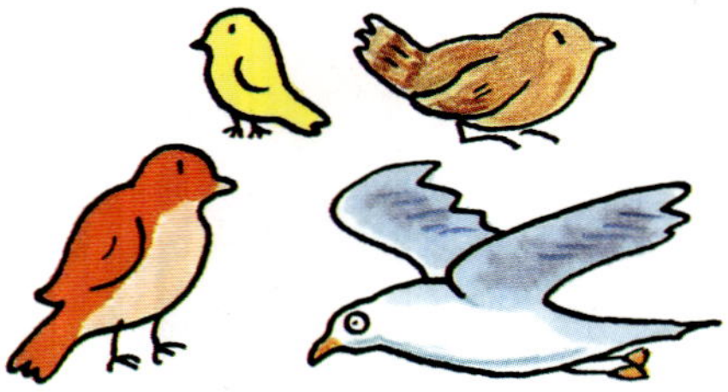

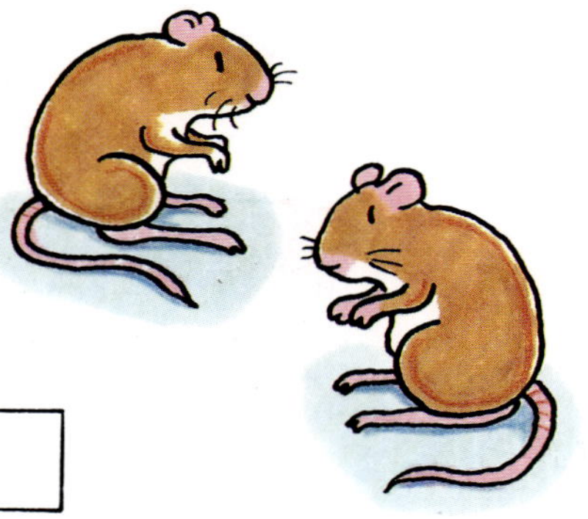

5 five

5 5 5 5 5 5 5

Count and colour

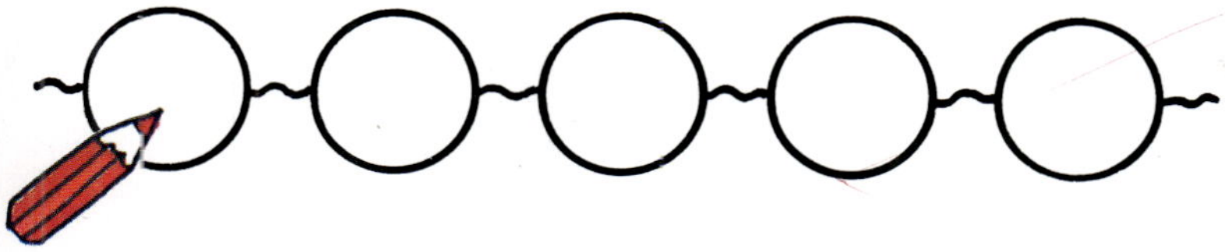

☐ 5 red

☐ blue

☐ green

☐ yellow

five   five   five

3 red   2 blue

Colour

2 red   3 blue

Count how many balls ☐

4 red   1 blue

Count how many balls ☐

1 one   2 two   3 three   4 four   5 five

 **4 and 1 more make 5 ice-creams**

Draw 2 more

Count     ⬜5

1   2   3   4   5

Draw 3 more

Count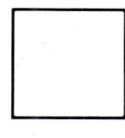

1   2

Draw 4 more

Count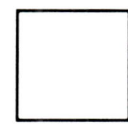

Draw 5 ice-creams

6 six

6 6 6 6 6 6

Count the sticks

☐ sticks  ☐ sticks

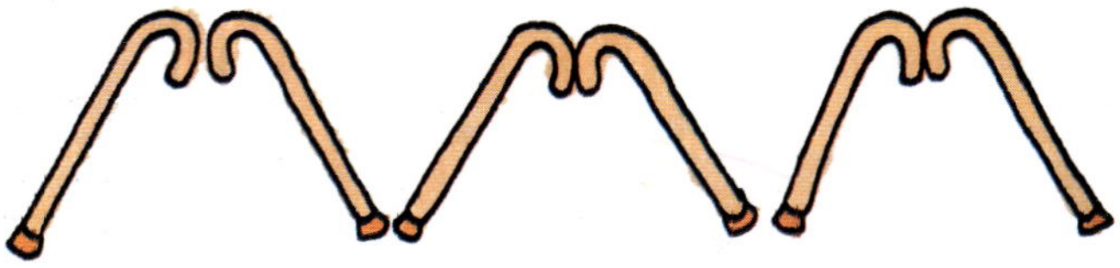

☐ sticks  ☐ sticks

☐ sticks 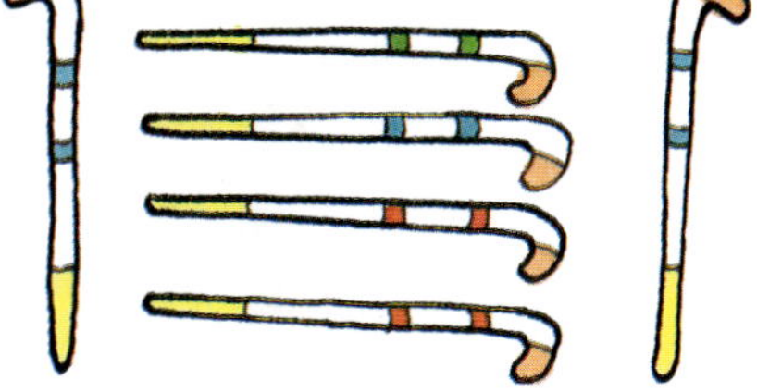 ☐ sticks

six six six six

Count the sheep

☐ sheep

☐ sheep

☐ sheep

☐ sheep

Draw 3 sheep

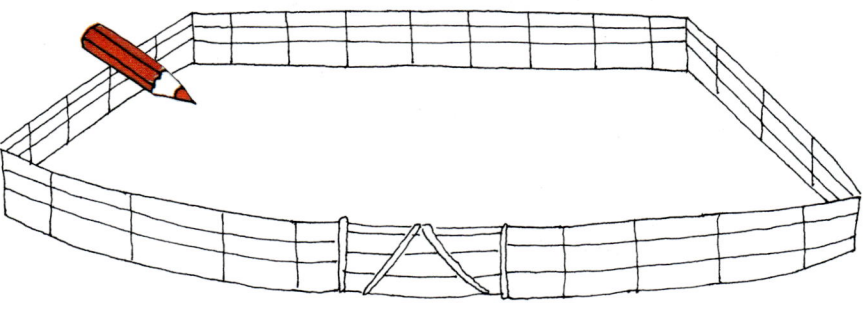

Sets

 4    3

Colour the sets

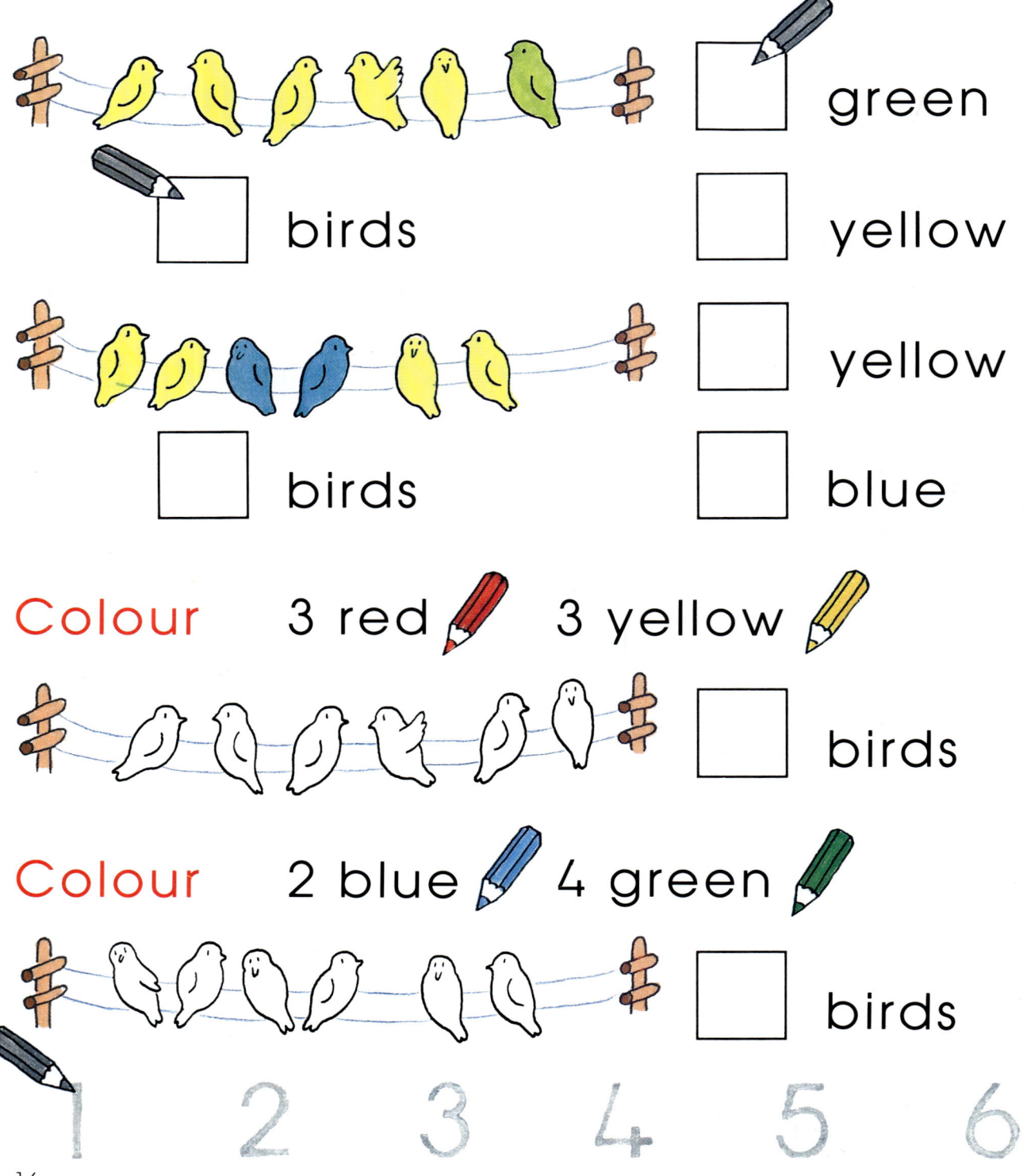

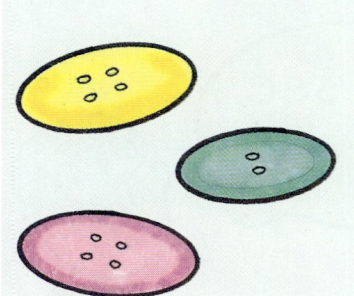 Colour the buttons

Colour

3 red
3 blue

4 red
2 blue

1 red
5 blue

2 red
4 blue

5 red
1 blue

6 red
0 blue

nought

one

17

3 birds   2 birds

"I can see 5 birds"

🐦🐦🐦🐦🐦 and 🐦 ☐ birds

🦜🦜🦜 and 🦜🦜 ☐ birds

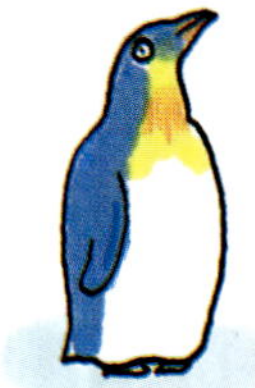

🐤🐤 and 🐤🐤🐤 ☐ birds

🐧 and 🐧🐧🐧🐧 ☐ birds

Draw round 5 birds

Add   3 + 1 = 4

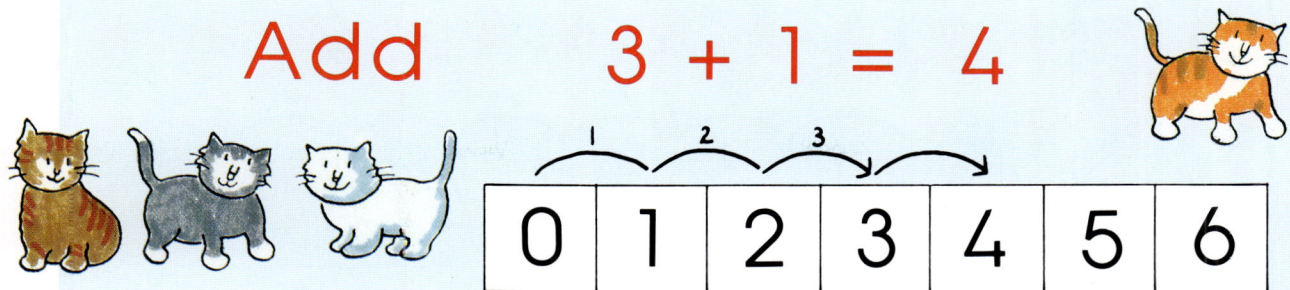

1 add 3 = ☐   2 add 2 = ☐

4 add 1 = ☐   5 add 0 = ☐

3 add 2 = ☐   1 add 4 = ☐

☐ add ☐ = ☐

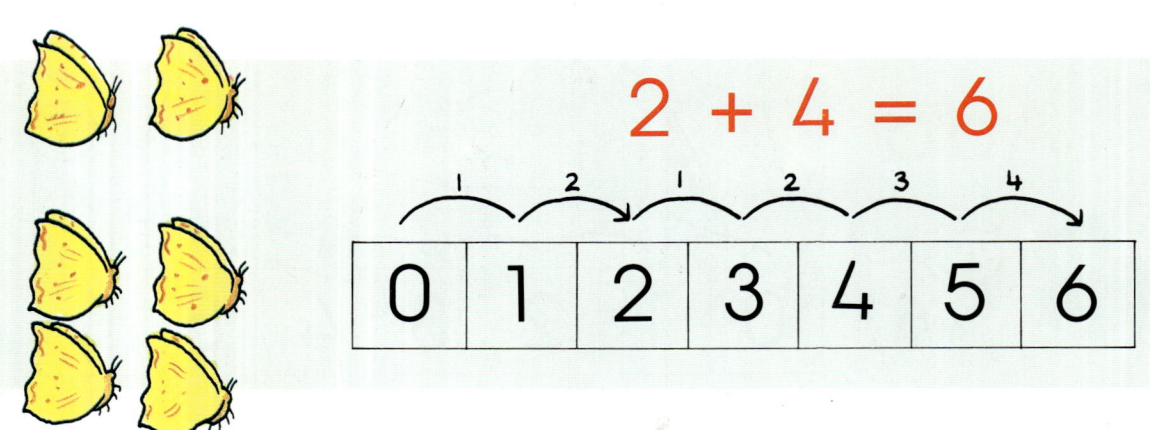

$2 + 4 = 6$

$5 + 1 = \square$

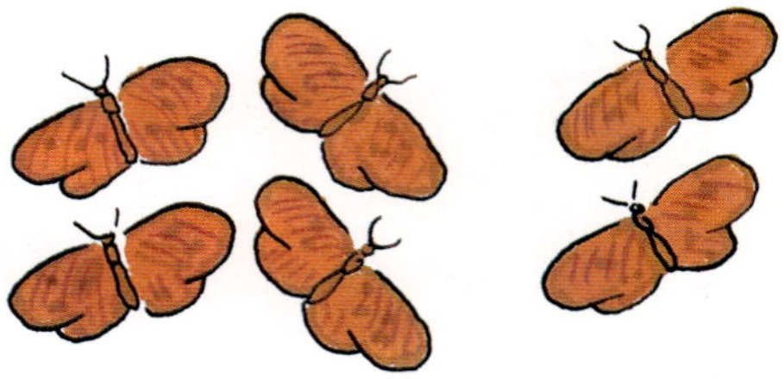

$4 + 2 = \square$

$3 + 3 = \square$

$2 + 4 = \square$

$6 + 0 = \square$

$1 + 5 = \square$

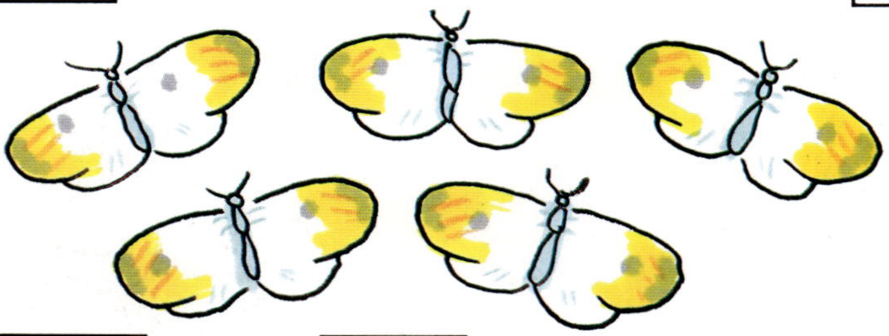

$\square + \square = \square$

Find the number

2 and ☐ make 3

3 and ☐ make 4

2 and ☐ make 4

1 and ☐ make 4

4 and ☐ make 5

2 and ☐ make 5

3 and ☐ make 5

1 and ☐ make 5

1 glove over

Join up

☐ rope over

☐ kite over

☐ dogs over

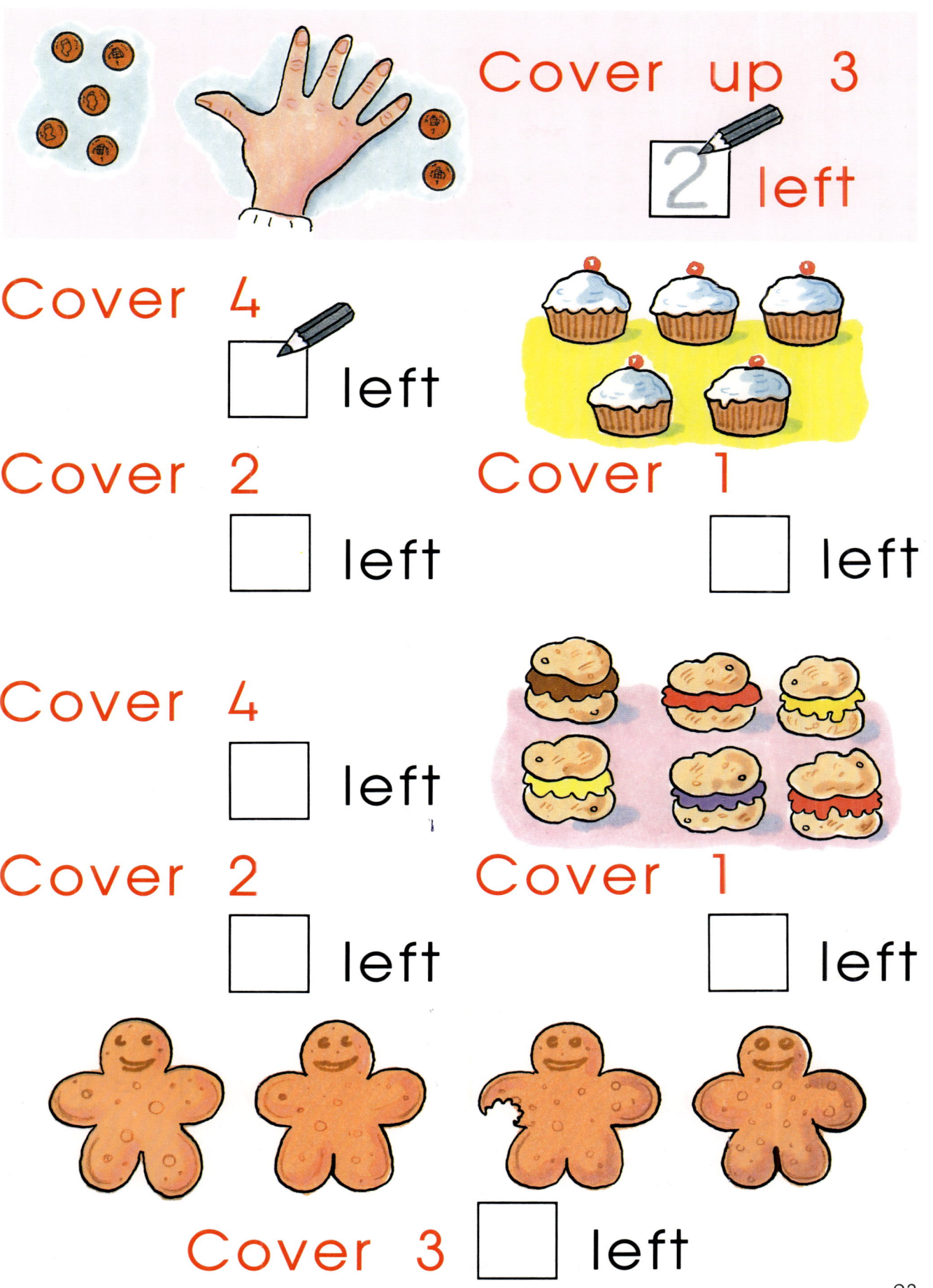

5 take away 2
= 3

3 take away 1 =

3 take away 2 =

3 take away 3 =

4 take away 1 =

4 take away 2 =

4 take away 3 =

4 take away 4 =

4 take away 0 =

5 ladybirds
3 fly away
2 left

4 take away 1 ☐ left

4 take away 2 ☐ left

4 take away 3 ☐ left

6 take away 1 ☐ left

6 take away 5 ☐ left

6 take away 4 ☐ left

6 take away 3 ☐ left

3 - 2 = 1

5 - 1 = ☐

5 - 2 = ☐

5 - 3 = ☐

5 - 4 = ☐

6 - 1 = ☐

6 - 2 = ☐

6 - 3 = ☐

6 - 4 = ☐

6 - 5 = ☐   6 - 6 = ☐

Money

spend 1p
☐ p left

spend 2p
☐ p left

spend 2p
☐ p left

spend 3p
☐ p left

spend 2p
☐ p left

spend 3p
☐ p left

spend 4p
☐ p left

spend 5p
☐ p left

Square  6 squares

Count the squares

Make some shapes

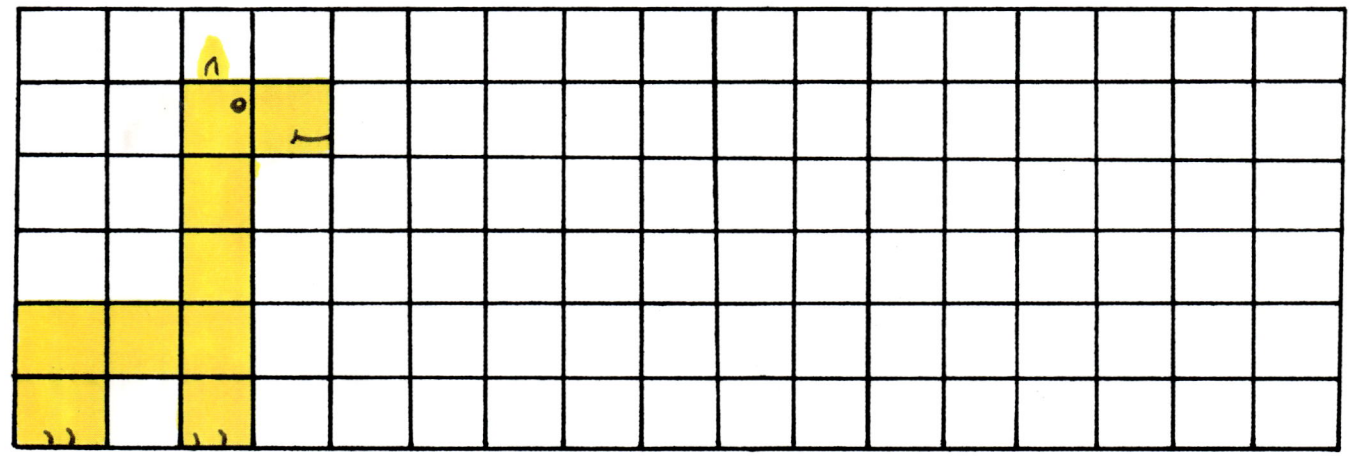

Cube

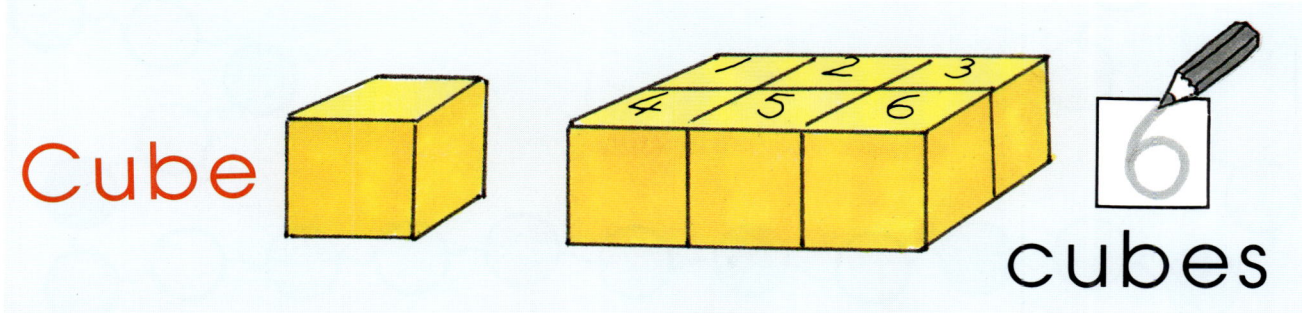 6 cubes

Count the cubes

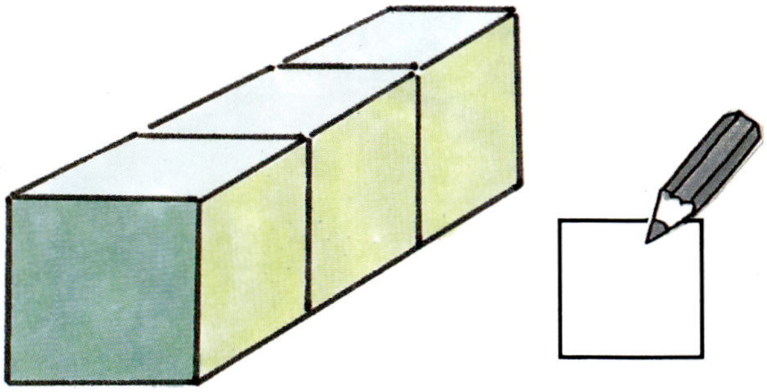

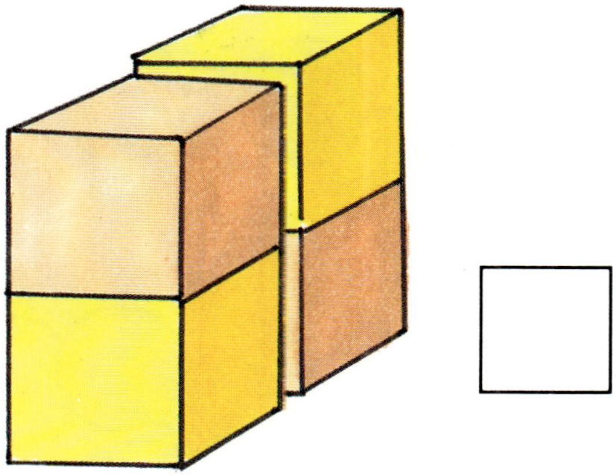

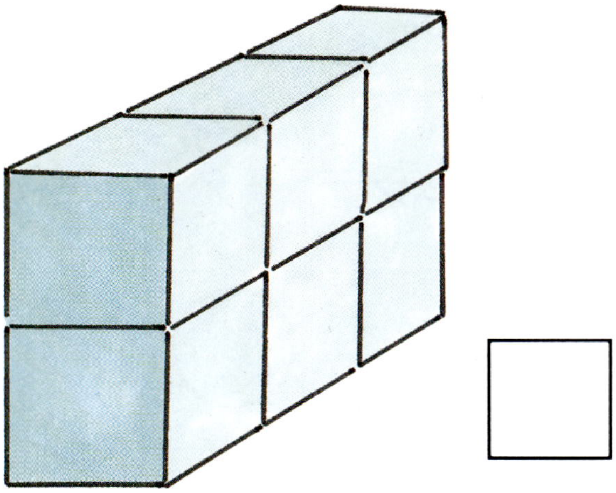

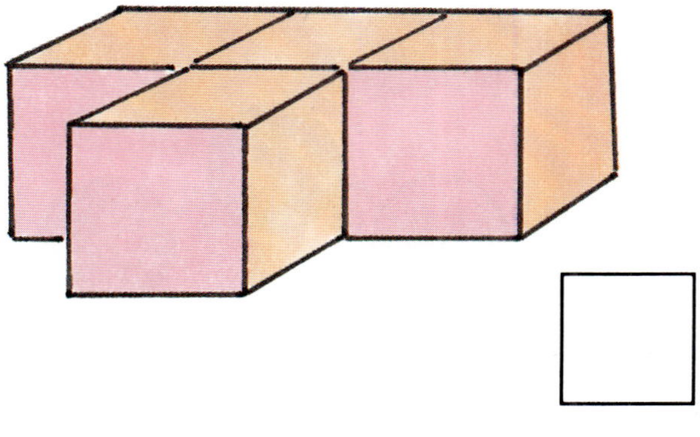

Use some of these to make shapes

Beads

Continue the patterns

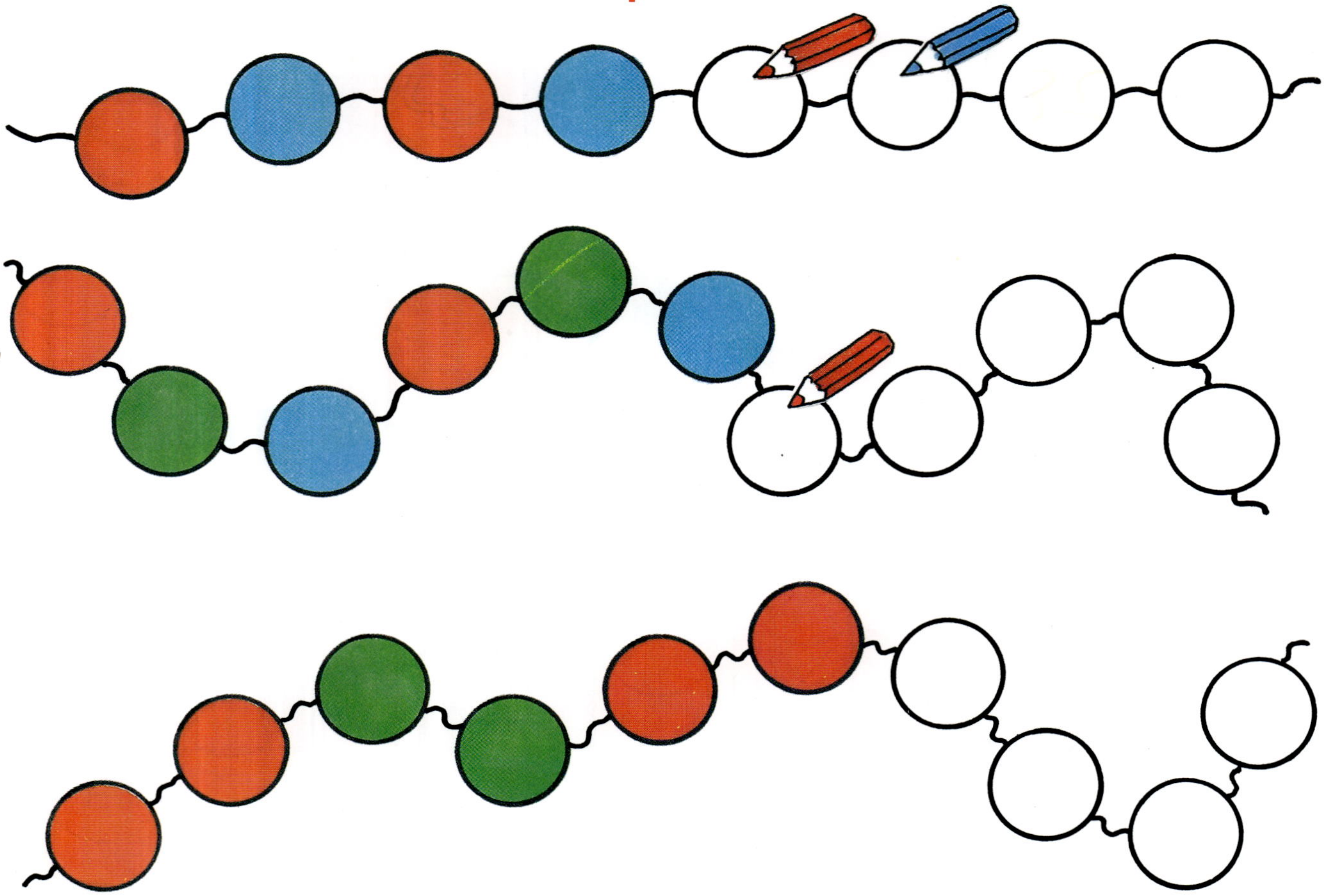

Make a pattern

Shapes

Continue the patterns

Use shapes to make patterns

Colour your patterns

Join up

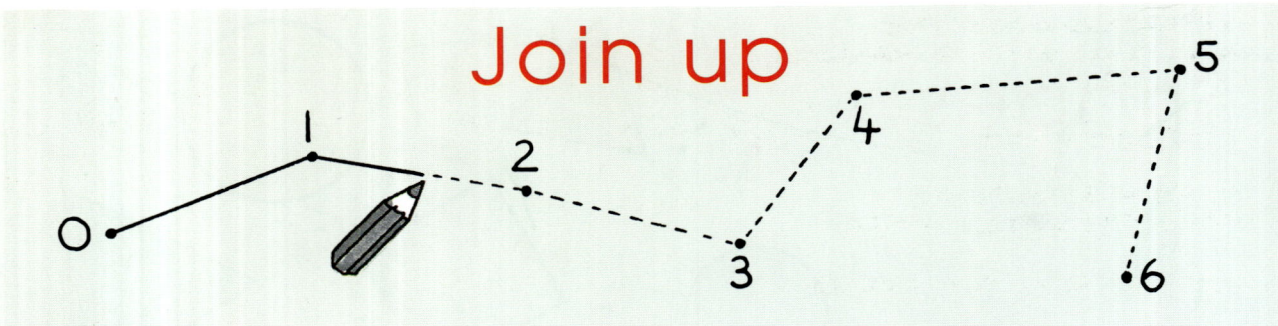

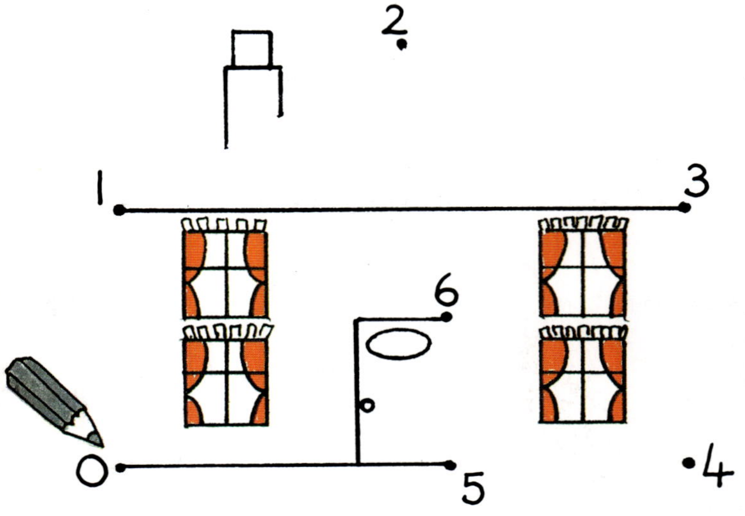

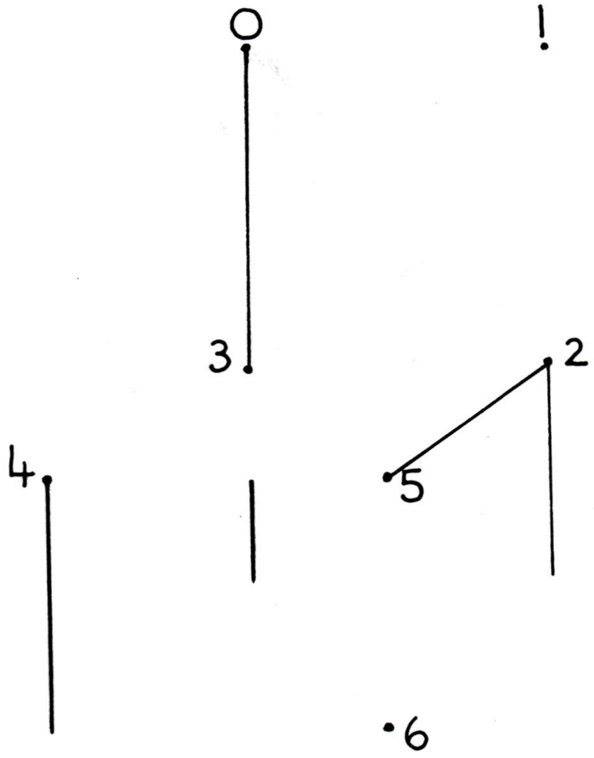

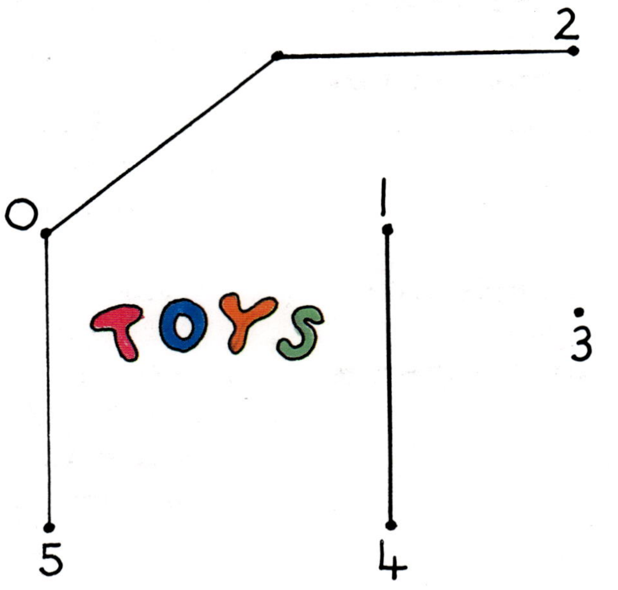